CHOOSE YOUR OWN CAREER ADVENTURE

NASA

Don Rauf

Created and produced by
Bright Futures Press, Cary, North Carolina
www.brightfuturespress.com

Published by
Cherry Lake Publishing, Ann Arbor, Michigan
www.cherrylakepublishing.com

Photo Credits: cover, Shutterstock/Castleski; page 5, Shutterstock/sripfoto; page 5, Shutterstock/Rachel Sanderoff; page 5, Shutterstock/Triff; page 7, Shutterstock/Andrey Armyagov; page 9, NASA; page 9, NASA; page 9, Shutterstock/Triff; page 11, NASA; page 13, Shutterstock/Marc Wood; page 13, Shutterstock/Vadim Sadovski; page 13, Shutterstock/Triff; page 15, NASA; page 17, NASA; page 17, NASA, page 17, Shutterstock/Triff; page 19, NASA; page 21, NASA; page 21, NASA; page 21, Shutterstock/Triff; page 23, NASA; page 25, NASA; page 25, page Shutterstock/Henrik Lehnerer; 25, Shutterstock/Triff; page 27, Shutterstock/Dmitry Zimin; 29, NASA; page 29, NASA; page 29, Shutterstock/Triff; page 31, NASA.

Library of Congress Cataloging-in-Publication Date

CIP has been filed and is available at catalog.loc.gov.

Printed in the United States of America.

Blast Off!

Welcome to America's premier space agency! NASA, the National Aeronautics and Space Administration, is the place where seemingly impossible quests into outer space become possible. It started in 1958 when NASA launched its first **satellite** into **orbit**. The next bold move was sending manned spacecraft to circle the earth. Then, in 1969, the whole world watched in wonder as the first men landed on the moon, walked around on it, and returned safely to Earth.

NASA continues its awe-inspiring missions today. **Astronauts** live for months at a time aboard the **International Space Station**, and space **rovers** explore Mars. Thanks to technologies like the Hubble telescope, scientists discover more about the universe every day.

It's easy to see why NASA is one of America's coolest places to work. It also puts a whole new spin on the term "work *space*"!

Get acquainted with some space-age opportunities. Pick your favorite career and let your NASA adventures begin!

TABLE OF CONTENTS

If you want to...		Go to page...
Blast off into outer space	Astronaut	5
Cook up some out-of-this-world food	Intergalactic Chef	9
Take a spin on the Red Planet	Mars Rover Driver	13
Call the shots from here on planet Earth	Mission Control Operator	17
Build a rocket bound for Mars	Rocket Scientist	21
Make a fashion statement in outer space	Space Suit Designer	25
Imagine your future in outer space	Write Your Own Career Adventure	29
Get some help with tricky words	Glossary	31
Locate specific information in this book	Index	32

ASTRONAUT

Astronaut needed for six-month mission aboard the International Space Station. Transportation provided aboard a rocket that blasts from 0 to 17,500 miles an hour in eight and a half minutes. Duties include living, working, and exploring on a spacecraft that orbits Earth every 90 minutes. Job involves working with other astronauts from around the world.

- *Ready to take on this challenge?*
  Turn to page 6.

- *Want to explore a career as an Intergalactic Chef instead?*
  Go to page 9.

- *Rather consider other choices?*
  Return to page 4.

Blast off for some online space exploration at www.nasa.gov/audience/forkids/kidsclub/flash.

Congratulations!

NASA officials just picked a new team of astronauts to send to the International Space Station—and guess what? You made the list! There is no need to pack your bags just yet. It will first take two years of super intense training to get ready.

Beware Microgravity!

One of your biggest challenges as an astronaut is learning to live with very little **gravity**. The 925,000-pound (419,573 kilograms) space station travels at a superfast speed of about 5 miles (8 kilometers) per second. At the same time, gravity pulls it toward Earth's surface. The result is a condition called **microgravity**. This is why people and objects seem weightless in space. Floating around all the time can be kind of fun. But it takes practice to get used to it.

Fortunately, NASA offers a great crash course in microgravity. Step aboard the **Vomit Comet**. It's a special aircraft where you will experience the joys of **weightlessness**. It won't take long to figure out how this training aircraft got its nickname. It moves very fast, then plunges for short periods of about 25 seconds. During these plunges, you feel weightless and, um, you might feel a little sick. Don't worry, though. It comes stocked with plenty of barf bags!

Space Travel Under the Sea

You passed all your training classes with flying colors! Now it's time for a test run. You won't be going up into outer space, not yet. You'll be heading down about 62 feet (19 meters) beneath the surface of the ocean. For the next three weeks, you will live aboard the Aquarius Reef Base laboratory.

Aquarius is the world's only undersea research station. Aquarius is located a few miles off the coast of Florida and is part of NASA's Extreme Environment Mission Operations program (NEEMO). Its habitat provides a convincing substitute for space exploration , as astronauts simulate living on a spacecraft. And it's a lot easier to get there!

Ready for Blastoff?

Your months of training fly by. You work hard and learn much. You are now a well-trained astronaut. The only thing left to do is buckle up, wave good-bye, and blast off!

Your Astronaut Career Adventure Starts Here

EXPLORE IT!

Use your Internet search skills to complete the following statements:

The International Space Station is ...

Microgravity is ...

My favorite NASA mission so far is ...

TRY IT!

Name Your Dream Team

If you could pick the people you would be spending six months cooped up with in the crowded confines of the International Space Station, who would you recruit? Make a list of seven people (friend, family, or famous) you'd want on your crew.

Out-of-This-World Fun

You will be spending months in outer space. No malls. No movie theaters. No friends to hang out with. Sure, you have a job to do, but you'll also have time off. Lots of it. What will you do to keep yourself entertained? Make a master list of the books, movies, and music you'll want to download on your tablet.

INTERGALACTIC CHEF

NASA looking for **food scientists** with out-of-this-world gourmet ideas that meet five intergalactic conditions: 1) Is it edible 18 months after you make it? 2) Is it easy to prepare in confined quarters? 3) Can astronauts eat it without making a mess in a microgravity environment? 4) Is it flavored strongly enough to taste good in space? 5) Does it provide the extra nutrition astronauts need to stay healthy?

- *Ready to take on this challenge?*
  Turn to page 10.

- *Want to explore a career as a Mars Rover Driver instead?*
  Go to page 13.

- *Rather consider other choices?*
  Return to page 4.

Dig in to some cosmic cuisine at www.nasa.gov/audience/forstudents/postsecondary/features/F_Food_for_Space_Flight.html.

Welcome to the NASA Kitchen!

It looks like a decked-out kitchen you'd find in any upscale gourmet restaurant. But the meals here aren't served to hungry customers who dine at tables. These meals will be eaten by astronauts orbiting some 225 miles (362 km) above Earth in the International Space Station. It's a place where microgravity changes everything—including the way food can be stored, prepared, and eaten.

Microgravity even affects the way food tastes. Astronauts report that their sense of taste is off in outer space. Food just isn't as flavorful up there. *Note to self: Crank up the spices!*

But before planning meals, you need to get acquainted with the astronauts you will be feeding during their mission in space. What kinds of foods do they like to eat? It doesn't take long to identify their favorites. Pizza and burritos!

Pizza is out. It needs to be refrigerated to stay fresh, but there are no refrigerators in space. They take up too much room and use too much energy. That's why astronauts can't keep fresh fruit and vegetables up there, either. Most of the food astronauts eat up there must be rehydrated using hot or cold water. They use a small oven to heat their meals when necessary.

Prep Time

The astronauts like your idea for a shrimp and bean burrito. You can preserve the food through a special process called **thermostabilization**. That destroys harmful microorganisms and helps keep food from going bad. You cook the shrimp and **irradiate** it so it will keep. The last thing astronauts need to deal with in space is smelly shrimp.

You'll have to experiment with different spices to give the burritos a pleasant burst of flavor. Then you have to figure out how to package it in a heatable foil-lined pouch that meets NASA's strict freshness standards. Now you are ready for a taste test.

You wrap shrimp, beans, and hot sauce in tortillas. Tortillas are great because they don't make crumbs like bread does. Crumbs can float off into equipment and cause problems. Tortillas also hold all the food inside so it doesn't float away.

It's time for the crew members to try your Burrito Loco. When they ask for seconds, you know it's a hit!

Your Intergalactic Chef Career Adventure Starts Here

EXPLORE IT!

Use your Internet search skills to find out more about the following:

The history of food in space from Tang! to Space Food Sticks

Meals Ready to Eat (MREs)

The first pizza delivery to the International Space Station

TRY IT!

What's on Your Space Menu?

Imagine you're chowing down up in space. What kinds of foods would you want to eat if you were far, far from home? Make a list of your top 10 food choices. Then think about the five big rules a NASA chef must follow. Which foods would make the cut? And remember: no crumbs!

Think to the Future

Astronauts plan their meals months in advance. If they can do it, so can you. Take a calendar and try planning what you will eat for a month. Write down what foods you think you might like to eat on, say, Tuesday three weeks from now. Include in your meal plans healthful foods that will energize you, and also vow to try new cuisines!

MARS ROVER DRIVER

Drivers wanted for Mars Exploration Rover. Driver's license not required, but experience driving remote-control cars and playing lots of video games useful. Vehicle is located 150 million miles (241 million km) away on the planet Mars. All driving done from a sophisticated, remote-control station on Earth. Scientifically-minded candidate looking for a long-distance adventure preferred.

- *Ready to take on this challenge?*
  Turn to page 14.

- *Want to explore a career as a Mission Control Operator instead?*
  Go to page 17.

- *Rather consider other choices?*
  Return to page 4.

Find the latest news about NASA's Mars Exploration Rover Mission at **mars.nasa. gov/mer/home**.

Start Your Engines

Get used to the idea of working on Mars. You will spend a lot of time there as part of NASA's **Mars Science Laboratory** (MSL) mission. You won't actually be on the Red Planet itself, however. You'll explore Mars by remote control from planet Earth. The key to this exploration is a six-wheeled car-sized rover named *Curiosity*. It's the next best thing to sending humans to explore!

You train for months on a simulator to learn how to operate the rover. Afterward as you get to know *Curiosity* better, you are surprised at how similar it is to a living creature. The rover has a "body," which protects its vital insides, and computer "brains" that process information. Cameras act a bit like a "head and neck" to give it a human-scale view of the planet's terrain. It has robotic limbs for exploring and wheeled "feet" to get it where it needs to go. It can even speak and listen.

Curiosity has been wandering around Mars since it was launched on November 26, 2011. Now it's your job to control it through powerful radio signals, computers, and monitors. The signals reach the rover through an advanced communication system called the **Deep Space Network**. You tell the rover where to go and what to do. The system works amazingly well.

Sometimes things get tricky, like when *Curiosity* is headed toward a cliff. Since it takes an average of 20 minutes for your signals to reach the rover, you have to pay attention at all times. The last thing you want to do is doze off and destroy a $2.5 billion space mission!

That's why a big part of your job is studying maps of the planet and carefully planning the rover's journey for the next day—although the rover can only travel about 660 feet each day. Your vehicle may have tough wheels but it's a tough planet. You have to be extra careful.

As the rover moves along, you capture images of the planet. You also send signals to guide its robotic arm to drill into the surface of Mars and collect samples. You work advanced instruments on board the rover to analyze the chemical makeup of these samples.

Your work pays off as NASA learns more about Mars. Someday humans might explore or even live on Mars, thanks to the discoveries you make with *Curiosity*.

Your Mars Rover Driver Career Adventure Starts Here

EXPLORE IT!

Use your Internet search skills to find out if any of these exist:

Water on Mars

Breathable air on Mars

Weather that humans can survive in on Mars

TRY IT!

Your Mars Survival Plan

What if you somehow got stranded on Mars? How would you survive? Think about ways you could get the basics that humans need to live.

Air	*Food*
Water	*Power*
Shelter	*Warmth*

Take a Rover for a Spin

Here's your chance to test drive a Mars rover. Go online to **www.nasa.gov/ externalflash/m2k4/driverover/frameset.html** and use your computer to steer the vehicle.

MISSION CONTROL OPERATOR

NASA seeking cool, calm, and collected communicator for **mission control** at Lyndon B. Johnson Space Center in Houston, Texas. Duties include monitoring astronauts on Orion mission attempting to land on an **asteroid**. The situation could get tense, but communicator cannot. Ideal position for person with his or her head in the clouds but feet on the ground.

- *Ready to take on this challenge?* Turn to page 18.

- *Want to explore a career as a Rocket Scientist instead?* Go to page 21.

- *Rather consider other choices?* Return to page 4.

Take command and see how mission control works at **spaceflight. nasa.gov/shuttle/ reference/mcc/index. html.**

Meteoric Rise

"*Orion*. This is Mission Control. Do you read me?"

You are behind a communications console at the Lyndon B. Johnson Space Center. This center manages flight controls for NASA's human space program. You are trying to communicate with astronauts who are on the first space journey to land on an asteroid. The astronauts' goal is to guide the asteroid along a different path. The mission hopes to learn how NASA can protect our planet if an enormous space rock ever takes aim at Earth.

You are part of a team of about 50 people working on the ground at mission control to support astronauts traveling in space. Your team works in shifts around the clock. Your team's success depends on technical knowledge, decisiveness, and communication.

It's been almost five minutes, and you haven't heard a reply. You are getting a little nervous. You check all systems for problems, but everything looks good. Why aren't the astronauts responding? You hold your breath ... until, finally, you hear the words you have been waiting for: "Yes, Houston. We read you."

You constantly check your monitors to make sure all systems are go. You keep track of power systems, fuel supplies, speed, direction, and weather patterns. Your team has a medical expert on staff, for consultation if any of the space crew has a physical problem.

You sit behind a desk equipped with monitors, a computer, and audio communications equipment. The headset you wear lets you give and receive information to the astronauts.

Your team has practiced many times for this mission, working through every imaginable problem. You are trained to give precise responses and calmly deliver step-by-step instructions.

The astronauts are ready to land on the asteroid. They radio to you, "Do we have a go to execute landing procedure 2.0?"

You reply, "Yes, you have a go, *Orion*."

Mission Accomplished!

When the two astronauts land safely on the asteroid, the whole team cheers! You check all monitors. The spacecraft is safe. All of the astronauts' **vital signs** are A-OK.

Job well done!

Your Mission Control Operator Career Adventure Starts Here

EXPLORE IT!

Use your Internet search skills to answer the following questions:

Did Apollo 11 *astronaut Neil Armstrong really say, "One small step for man; one giant leap for mankind"?*

Why did Apollo 13 *astronaut Jack Swigert utter the now famous line, "Houston, we've had a problem"?*

What poem did President Ronald Reagan quote in his address to the nation after the explosion of the space shuttle Challenger?

TRY IT!

Find Your Way Home

Try writing down step-by-step directions on how to get from your house to your school. Ask your parent if the directions are correct.

Say What?

Astronauts and mission control use special phrases and words to communicate. What do you suppose the following phrases mean?

"Roger."	*"Over and out."*
"Mission critical."	*"Abort."*
"All systems are go."	*"T minus 5 minutes."*

ROCKET SCIENTIST

Rocket scientists needed to imagine, design, and build new spacecraft to travel farther and faster than any flight vehicle has ever flown. Responsible for inventing rocket ship and finding new fuel source that goes the distance for very deep space travel to Mars. Ideal candidate loves science and has an oversized sense of adventure.

- *Ready to take on this challenge?*
  Turn to page 22.

- *Want to explore a career as a Space Suit Designer instead?*
  Go to page 25.

- *Rather consider other choices?*
  Return to page 4.

Select a NASA mission, build a virtual rocket, and blast off at www. nasa.gov/externalflash/ RocketScience101/ RocketScience101.html.

It's Rocket Science, Really

Sometimes people joke about needing to be as smart as a rocket scientist to do a certain job. That's because rocket scientists are really, really smart. But this is no joke. NASA needs the smartest scientists they can find for their **Space Launch System** team.

The mission? Find a way to get astronauts to Mars and then get them safely back to Earth.

Using current rocket technology, it would take about seven months to get a spaceship to Mars. That's a very long time to be in flight! Even if that were possible, there's an even bigger problem to solve. No one yet knows how to get a rocket back to Earth once it lands on Mars.

As part of the Space Launch System team, you'll work on the biggest and most powerful rocket ever built. So far, the best idea NASA has had is to use a 5.75 million-pound (2.6 million kg) spacecraft that gets incredible thrust from engines that run on liquid hydrogen and oxygen. While this type of rocket could zoom at high speeds through space, it is not fast enough for this mission. Your team is exploring even faster ways to travel.

Now you are experimenting with a new engine that runs on a superheated gas called **plasma**. A plasma engine could cut a

Mars trip down to just about six weeks. In your modern lab, you have the computers and materials to design your rockets and research new ways for high-speed travel.

Rock It!

While you work on the engine, other team members work on making the spaceship comfortable for astronauts to live in. Astronauts will need places to work, sleep, eat, and relax while exploring Mars. A team member asks for your ideas about a space-age toilet. You strongly recommend adding straps so astronauts can fasten themselves to the seat. Microgravity is not something astronauts want to deal with when using the bathroom!

It will be a long time before this mission is complete. When it is, astronauts will go where no human has gone before. Mars, here we come!

Your Rocket Scientist Career Adventure Starts Here

EXPLORE IT!

Use your Internet search skills to complete the following statements:

Aerospace engineering is ...

The Space Launch System is ...

*Isaac Newton's Third Law of Motion explains how rockets move
in space by ...*

TRY IT!

Launch Your Own Rocket

Before you can design the rocket of the future, you need to know more
about rockets of the past. Explore the history of rockets and make a
timeline showing how they've changed over time.

Design Your Own Spacecraft

Draw a sketch of the inside of your ideal spaceship. What would your
sleeping area look like? What would be your concerns in making a kitchen
area? How would you keep things from floating? How would you keep
things compact and efficient so you don't waste space?

SPACE SUIT DESIGNER

Ready to make a fashion statement in outer space? NASA needs **space suit designers** to help astronauts dress for success on space missions. Ideal candidates have fashion sense and engineering smarts. Space suits must be fashioned to keep space travelers alive and well-protected while allowing for comfort and flexibility.

- *Ready to take on this challenge?*
  Turn to page 26.

- *Want to explore a career as an Astronaut instead?*
  Go to page 5.

- *Rather consider other choices?*
  Return to page 4.

Learn how space suits are constructed at http://bit.ly/NASASpacesuit.

Space Age Fashionista

NASA is impressed with your combined knowledge of fashion and engineering. Now you have to prove you've got what it takes to redesign space suits for 21st-century space travel.

Before you get started, you need to see the space suits that are currently in use. Wow! You didn't realize how BIG they are. It's like wearing a personal spacecraft. The big white suits astronauts wear outside the space station are called extravehicular mobility units, or EMUs. They are awkward and weigh about 280 pounds (127 kg). Microgravity is a good thing when your clothes weigh more than you do!

It's no wonder they are so heavy. They are equipped with voice, video, and data communications systems; medical monitoring systems; and sophisticated caution and warning systems.

Cosmic Comfort Zone

One of your challenges is to find a fabric that is flexible and light but also puncture-proof. You don't want the suit to tear if an astronaut gets hit by a meteoroid!

The new suit must also provide temperature control. Temperatures in space can get as hot as an oven—275 degrees

Fahrenheit (135 degrees Celsius)—in direct sunlight. With no sun, temperatures drop to hundreds of degrees below zero. Creating systems that withstand both extremes requires serious design ideas.

There are other things to think about too. For instance, the suit must connect to a backpack that holds a water tank (for drinking) and oxygen. It also needs a source of electricity. The fans that move oxygen through the suit need power. So do the lights, the communications system, and an **air pressure system**. Making sure these systems work without a glitch is a high priority. Without the right air pressure around the body, the fluids inside an astronaut would start to boil.

Don't forget to include several small thruster jets on the back of the new suit. That way, an astronaut who begins to drift away can jet back toward the spaceship. And be sure to figure out how astronauts can use the bathroom while in the suit.

It will take some time and a lot of work. But, hey, you've got this job sewn up!

Your Space Suit Designer Career Adventure Starts Here

EXPLORE IT!

Use your Internet search skills to complete the following statements:

Sometimes astronauts wear orange space suits because ...

The suits for working in space are white because ...

Astronauts communicate when wearing spaces suits by ...

TRY IT!

Sketch It Out

Draw your design for a modern space suit. It doesn't have to be scientifically accurate. Just keep in mind what space suits need to provide. Give it a try and be creative!

Layer It On Thick

Space suits have many layers for protection. Want to get an idea of what it would be like to wear a space suit? Put on at least four or five layers of clothing, and then try walking around the house and doing things. What does it feel like?

WRITE YOUR OWN CAREER ADVENTURE

WRITE YOUR OWN CAREER ADVENTURE

You just read cool details about six awesome NASA careers:

- Astronaut
- Intergalactic chef
- Mars rover driver
- Mission control operator
- Rocket scientist
- Space suit designer

Which one is your favorite? Pick one, and imagine what it might be like to do that job. Then write your own career adventure!

_____

_____

_____

_____

_____

_____

_____

_____

Go online to download free activity sheets at www.cherrylakepublishing.com/activities.

ATTENTION, ADVENTURERS! Please do NOT write in this book if it is not yours. Use a separate piece of paper.

GLOSSARY

air pressure system space suit system that creates the same pressure as the atmosphere on Earth's surface

asteroid large, rocky object that orbits the sun

astronaut person trained to work in a spacecraft

Deep Space Network system of large antennae and communications stations that NASA uses to contact and control spacecraft and satellites

food scientist person who studies the physical, biological, and chemical makeup of food

gravity force that attracts things toward the center of Earth, a planet, or any other physical body with mass

intergalactic relating to outer space or the space between galaxies

International Space Station large research center and science lab that orbits Earth

irradiate expose food to a controlled amount of energy called ionizing radiation, in order to preserve it

Mars rover driver professional on Earth who controls and drives the Mars rover via a long-distance communications system

Mars Science Laboratory robotic space probe mission to Mars launched by NASA on November 26, 2011, which successfully landed *Curiosity*, a robotic rover, in Gale Crater on August 6, 2012

meteoroid solid object moving through space, usually small and rocky or metallic, smaller than an asteroid but at least as big as a speck of dust

microgravity condition in which people or things appear to be weightless, such as astronauts floating in a spacecraft

mission control command center for directing, supporting, and monitoring a manned space mission

mission control operator person on Earth who communicates with astronauts and helps them with information, instructions, and technical issues

orbit regular, repeating path one object in space takes around another

plasma gas that is heated until the atoms lose all their electrons, leaving a highly electrified collection of nuclei and free electrons

rocket scientist scientist who designs and constructs rockets and other spacecraft, also known as an aerospace engineer

rover vehicle controlled by robotics and designed to explore the surface of Mars

satellite anything that orbits something else, also refers to a device that travels around Earth for communicating or collecting information

Space Launch System powerful, advanced launch vehicle for a new era of human exploration beyond Earth's orbit

space suit designer professional who uses fashion skills and scientific knowledge to construct space uniforms, also known as space suit engineers

thermostabilization preservation of food by heat, usually under pressure

thrust force that moves an aircraft through the air

Vomit Comet NASA program that introduces astronauts to the feeling of zero-gravity space flight

weightlessness having no apparent weight or gravitational pull

INDEX

A

aerospace engineering, 24
Apollo, 20
Aquarius, 7
Armstrong, Neil, 20
asteroid, 17
astronaut, 5

D

Deep Space Network, 14

E

Earth, 5

F

food scientist, 9

G

gravity, 6

I

intergalactic chef, 9
International Space Station, 5

L

Lyndon B. Johnson Space
  Center, 17

M

Mars, 3, 13
Mars rover, 16
Mars rover driver, 16
Meal Ready to Eat (MRE), 12
mission control operator, 17,
  20

N

NASA, 3
NEEMO (NASA's Extreme
  Environment Mission
  Operations), 7
Newton, Sir Isaac, 24

P

pizza, 10
plasma, 22

R

rocket, 22
rocket scientist, 22

S

satellite, 3
Space Food Sticks, 12
Space Launch System, 22,24
space suit designer, 25
Swigert, Jack, 20

T

Tang!, 12

V

Vomit Comet, 6

ABOUT THE AUTHOR

Don Rauf was the editor-in-chief of *Careers and Colleges* magazine. He has written more than 30 nonfiction books, mostly for children and young adults, including *Killer Lipstick and Other Spy Gadgets*, *The Rise and Fall of the Ottoman Empire*, and *Simple Rules for Card Games*. He lives in Seattle with his wife, Monique, and son, Leo.